井津 建郎
KENRO IZU

「アンコール遺跡　光と影」
"Light Over Ancient Angkor"

プラチナ・プリント
Platinum Prints

for Mr. & Mrs. Whiting

[signature] Sept. 17 '96

井津建郎さんのこと

細江 英公

　1990年夏、ニューヨークのソーホー地区にある写真専門の画廊ハワード・グリーンバーグ・ギャラリー(当時のフォトファインド・ギャラリー)でのことだった。画廊主が奥の引き出しから大事そうにそっと見せてくれたプラチナ・プリントの「花」、「エジプトのピラミッド」や「マヤの古代遺跡」、「イングランドのストーンヘンジ」などに、私は衝撃的ともいえる感動を覚えた。一点一点の作品はプラチナ・プリント特有の人間的な柔らかさ、美しさ、力強さ、繊細さと微妙さ、そして細密画より微細な大型密着プリントの超細密性、さらに優雅の極みともいえる温黒の色調など、まさに完璧そのものだった。そして、私は写真から放射されるアウラを一瞬に感じとり、作品の底に潜む深い精神性に胸を打たれたのである。

　私は同じ日本人の未だ見ぬ作者にすぐにでも会いたかったが、その時はお互いに時間がなくて、実際に会って話ができたのは翌年の、同じニューヨークだった。年齢をきくと42才(当時)という働き盛りの若さながら、もの静かで、丁寧な口調で話す物腰が印象的だった。話が弾むうちに私はこの写真家の内部に、底知れぬ忍耐力と、そして何よりも、写真に対する溢れるばかりの情熱を見いだしたのである。その時、私は16才も年下の井津さんに、尊敬の気持ちと同時に、20年来の友人のような親しみを感じたのだった。

　1991年、井津さんは日本ではじめての個展を、日本橋のツァイトフォトサロンで開いた。さらに翌年、同じギャラリーで開いた第2回展も大成功、ようやく日本において「井津建郎のプラチナ・プリント」の存在が知られるところとなった。

　以来、私はニューヨークに行くたびに井津さんのスタジオを訪れ、93年、94年、95年撮影のアンコールワットのほとんどのプリントを見せてもらったが、そのなかには現像したばかりのネガもあった。ネガといっても14×20インチの大きさがあり、私も同じプラチナ・プリントを手がける同輩として、そのネガがいかにプラチナ・プリントに最適な理想的濃度で、最高の出来映えであるかを知るだけに、そのネガからの仕上がりを想像して、胸のときめきを抑えることができなかった。

　あるとき私は井津さんに尋ねた。井津さんは1979年以来、石の遺跡を撮り続けてきたが、その動機と理由は、そしてなぜ、「石」なのか？と。井津さんは私の問いに対して、「何億年、何万年もの時間を通過してきた『石』の中に、生命の根源を見るからですよ。そして『石』の中には神が宿っていて、自然に吸い寄せられるのを肌で感じるんです‥」と。さらに続けて、アンコールの石はエジプトやマヤのピラミッド、イースター島の巨石などと同じ石でも違う

という。それまでは対象に対して畏怖の感情があったが、アンコールではそれまでの他の遺跡では知らなかった「やすらぎ」を感じたという。それはなぜか分からないが、今までと同じ気持ちで、一枚一枚、祈りながら撮らせていただきましたと、事もなげに語ってくれた。これこそは、敬虔な仏師が仏像を彫刻するとき、一刀一刀刻むたびに、三たび礼拝するという「一刀三礼」の尊い精神である。

　1992年、井津さんはスイスの写真家マルク・リブが撮ったアンコール・ワットの写真をふと見て、その瞬間、無性に現地に行きたくなったという。その頃、カンボジアの治安は悪く危険だから行くなという家族や回りの友人たちの反対を押しきって、何ものかに憑かれたように現地に入ったそうだ。一人で100キロ近くのカメラ機材を運び、ただ現地のガイドと運転手だけのチームで、戦乱の硝煙が消えない危険地帯の只中で寺院の写真を撮るために。それはまるで気違いじみた自殺行為と言われても仕方がない。しかし、アンコールの石の空間に身を置いてると、むしろ「やすらぎ」を感じて怖いと思ったことは一度もなかったと井津さんはいう。それでも撮影中に、ロケット砲を背負った兵士に金を出せと脅かされ、言われるままに金をだしたら、今度は自分たちが守ってやるといって外敵の攻撃から守ってくれたそうだ。そんな時、井津さんは地雷を踏んで足をなくした子供たちがカメラの回りで遊んでいる姿を目の当たりにして、何とかこの子供たちを救う手だてはないだろうかとそれだけを考えたという。井津建郎さんとはそういう写真家なのだ。

・　・　・

　このたびの井津建郎プラチナ・プリント新作展「アンコール遺跡光と影」は、清里フォトアートミュージアムの基本理念である〈生命(いのち)あるものへの共感〉に添うまことに意義ある展覧会であり、しかも、これから日本各地そして世界各国の巡回に先駆けて、まず最初に本ミュージアムで展覧する名誉をいただきました。関係者を代表して作者の井津建郎さんに感謝いたします。また、井津さんはこれを機会に、アンコールの村に子供たちのための病院を建設するための基金「アンコール・チャイルド・クリニック・ファンド」を設立されました。私たちはこの基金が一日でも早く目標に達することを微力ながら支援したいと思います。

　最後になりましたが、本展図録のために特別にご執筆いただきました梅棹忠夫先生、石澤良昭先生に厚く御礼申し上げます。

清里フォトアートミュージアム館長

On Kenro Izu and His Platinum Prints

Eikoh Hosoe

It was in the summer of 1990 at the Howard Greenberg Gallery in the Soho district of New York (it was called the Photofind Gallery at that time). The gallery owner took these platinum prints out from a special drawer: Flower, Egyptian Pyramid, Ancient Mayan Ruins, England's Stonehenge. I remember being deeply moved by the special human feeling of the platinum prints, their beauty and power together with subtlety and delicacy like the quiver of a tremolo, and their extraordinary detail and elegant accents in warm black hues, all in harmonious perfection. For an instant I perceived an aura projected from the surface of the photographs and a fathomless feeling of spirituality came over me.

Since he was a fellow Japanese and an artist whom I had not seen, I wanted to meet him right away, but since neither of us had time, we did not actually meet and talk until the following year in New York. At the time he was 42, and while brimming with an industriousness of youth, he had such serenity that I began to wonder where he managed to conceal his energy. Only as the conversation proceeded did Izu's boundless tenacity and overflowing passion for photography emerge. From that point I felt a respect for Izu and an intimacy one might expect from a twenty-year friendship.

In 1991 Izu opened his first solo exhibition in Japan at the Zeit Foto Salon in Nihonbashi, Tokyo. Then in 1992 with the great success of his second exhibition at the Zeit Foto Salon, Izu's platinum prints finally gained recognition in Japan.

After that, I visited Izu's studio every time I was in New York. He showed me almost every print he made of Angkor Wat from '93, '94 and '95, and some of the negatives he had only just developed. These negatives measure 14 by 20 inches, and as someone who has experience with the platinum printing process, I could tell that they were ideal. Just seeing the quality of the negatives and imagining the finished prints, I could hardly contain my excitement.

I questioned Izu. Why had he been photographing stone ruins since 1979? Because of the stone? He told me, "I feel that life's source can be found in stones that have existed for hundreds of millions of years. I sense the gods' presence in stones and I am naturally drawn to them." Moreover, the Angkor stones were the same as those of the Egyptian or Mayan pyramids, or the great stones of Easter Island, and yet they were different. Up until then, he had felt a sense of awe toward the objects, but at Angkor he felt a tranquility that he had never known from the other sites. And though he does not know why, with the same feeling as before, he told me casually that he said a prayer with each exposure. This is the same noble spirit by which the pious carver of Buddha images makes three prayers for each stroke of his carving tool.

Izu felt an overwhelming compulsion to go and photograph Angkor Wat after seeing the work of Swiss photographer Marc Riboud in 1992. At that time the political situation was unstable and he was warned of the danger. Over the objections of his family, as if possessed by spirits, he went to Cambodia. Carrying nearly 200 pounds of camera equipment and traveling with a team consisting of only a local driver and guide, he entered war-torn Cambodia. With gunpowder still lingering in the air, photographing Cambodia was almost suicidal. On the contrary, his enchantment with the stone monuments of Angkor enveloped him more in tranquility than fear. While photographing Angkor Wat, Izu was approached by a soldier carrying a rocket launcher on his back. The soldier demanded money. When Izu complied the soldier promised to defend him and apparently did provide protection during an excursion. But more than that, Izu's mind was on the local children who had lost legs by stepping on mines. Izu saw these children playing around his camera equipment and he began to wonder if something couldn't be done for them. Kenro Izu is that kind of photographer.

• • •

Last year Izu started the "Angkor Child Clinic Fund" to raise money to build a clinic for the village children of Angkor. We sincerely wish him well in the early attainment of his funding goals. "Light Over Ancient Angkor" is an exhibit of Kenro Izu's new platinum prints, and I believe it is especially fitting to this museum's theme of "sympathy with all forms of life." We are honored to have this museum chosen for the first exhibit before his work moves on to other locations in Japan and overseas. On behalf of the museum staff, I would like to express my appreciation.

I would like to take this opportunity to express my gratitude to Mr. Tadao Umesao for providing his insightful essay, and to Professor Yoshiaki Ishizawa for providing valuable information, for this book.

Director, Kiyosato Museum of Photographic Arts

石造りの遺跡に魅せられて

井津 建郎

過去17年にわたり、エジプト、シリア、ヨルダン、メキシコ、チリ（イースター島）、イギリス、スコットランド、フランス、ビルマ、ベトナム、インドネシア、そしてカンボジアを撮影し続けてきました。

石造遺跡に感じる神性および、それを包む空間密度の定着には、大型原寸大ネガによる密着プラチナ・プリント技法以外には私には考えられませんでした。

そして、それは、特注製作した超大型カメラ(14×20インチ)を背に、古代遺跡をとおして私の心に響く「何か」を求めての行脚でもあります。

過去3年間、5度にわたるアンコール遺跡群の撮影を通して、今までにない「何か大切なもの」を、ひとつ、そこで学ばせてもらったような気がします。
半ば廃墟と化した寺の中に立つ時、心に感じる温もり、風化しかけて土との境目のわからなくなっている基石を見る時の安らぎさは、一体何なのだろうかと今でも考えます。

また、この数度の旅を通じて、カンボジアでは1940年代以来、凡そ800万個にものぼる地雷が埋められ、4万人を越える一般市民が死亡あるいは負傷し、今日でも平均1日1人が犠牲者となっていること、特に、野原で働き、遊ぶ子供たちが犠牲となることも少なくない、ということを知りました。

アンコール遺跡群から学ばせてもらった感謝の気持ちを、このアンコールの村に何かの形で表現したい、との思いがつのり、私のアンコール遺跡全作品の売り上げをカンボジアの子供達の病院建設・運営資金とする、「アンコール・チャイルド・クリニック・ファンド」の企画に到りました。

この企画を通じて、たくさんの心優しい人々と巡り会うことができました。様々な方面から支持・援助をいただき、少しずつですが、「アンコール・チャイルド・クリニック・ファンド」が動き始めています。
世界的なスケールから見れば、ささやかなプロジェクトですが、世界の人びとがみな友人となる平和な日を迎えるための一歩ともなれば、と祈っています。

清里フォトアートミュージアムの細江英公館長には、数年前初めてニューヨークで拙作をご覧いただいて以来、暖かいご支持をいただき、この企画を話した折りも、即座に主旨にご賛同いただきました。「アンコール遺跡　光と影」展の実現には、細江館長の多大なお力添えをいただきましたことにたいし、ここに改めて感謝の念を表したいと存じます。

1996年3月

Light and Shadow of The Angkor

Kenro Izu

Over my 17-year enchantment with stone monuments, I have made photographs in Egypt, Syria, Jordan, Mexico, Chile (Easter Island), England, Scotland, France, Burma, Vietnam, Indonesia, and Cambodia. To capture the spirituality I feel in stone remains and the density of atmosphere that embraces them, I can think of no other medium than platinum prints made by contact printing with large format negatives.

As I walk among the antiquities with a large, custom made camera strapped on my back, I am on a pilgrimage in search of something that touches my heart. In the course of five photography excursions over the past three years I feel now that there is some spiritual essence that I am meant to learn. Standing in time worn temples, I get a warm, peaceful feeling from seeing the weathered foundation stones blend seamlessly with earth. Still the peacefulness I sense from these ruins puzzles me.

In my travels, I learned that some eight million mines have been buried in Cambodia since 1940, and that over 40 thousand civilians have been killed or injured by them. Even today, on average, these mines claim one new victim every day, and the victims are often children who work and play in the fields.

Thinking that I wanted to somehow express my appreciation for all that the Angkor ruins have taught me, I decided to contribute all the proceeds from my Angkor works for the construction and operation of a children's clinic. Toward that end, the "Angkor Child Clinic Fund" was created.

In creating this fund, I have had the opportunity to meet a great many gracious people. I have received support and assistance from all quarters, and the "Angkor Child Clinic Fund" has gradually gotten underway. Though this project is modest on a world scale, I hope it will be a step toward peace and friendship among the world's people.

Since Mr. Eikoh Hosoe was kind enough to view my work in New York some years ago, he has been a source of warm support, and as the director of the Kiyosato Museum of Photographic Arts, he has given his unhesitating endorsement for this project. I would like to take this opportunity to express my appreciation for his assistance in making this exhibition possible.

March 1996

アンコール・ワットと祇園精舎

梅棹 忠夫

1860年、フランスの探検家アンリ・ムオーは、カンボジアの西北部の密林のなかに、壮麗な石造建築物が存在することを「発見」した。これがいわゆる「アンコール・ワットの発見」である。この寺の存在は一部のヨーロッパ人たちにはすでに知られていたが、ムオーの記述がヨーロッパに紹介されて有名になったのである。

この付近に住むカンボジアの人たちは、この巨大な建築物の存在をもちろんよく知っていた。ましてや土にうもれていたものを発掘したわけではない。森林にかこまれていたというだけであって、建造物自体は地上に姿をあらわしていたのである。

1957年の秋、わたしははじめてこの壮麗な寺院をおとずれた。そして、翌年の春にもここにいった。この二どにわたる訪問の結果いえるたしかなことは、アンコール・ワットは遺跡ではないということである。これは生きて機能している寺院なのである。現に南方上座部仏教の僧たちが住み、線香の煙がたえることがない信仰の場なのである。このような生きている宗教施設を遺跡あつかいすることはできない。

アンコール・ワットが建造されたのは12世紀の初頭のことである。当時カンボジアの王であったスーリヤヴァルマン2世によって、約30年の歳月をかけて造営されたものである。アンコール・ワットに隣接して、アンコール・トムの遺跡がある。これはたしかに住むひともない遺跡であって、一群の石造建造物がのこっている。このアンコール・トムは、当時のアンコール朝クメール帝国の王宮であって、12世紀末から13世紀にかけて、クメールの王ジャヤヴァルマン7世によって造営されたものである。これが、当時インドシナ半島において勢威をふるったアンコール朝クメール国家の首都だったのである。わたしはジープを駆ってこれらの遺跡をまわったが、広大な森林の各所に遺跡が散在し、ひととおり見るだけでも一日仕事であった。

アンコール・ワットにもどろう。この巨大な寺院は四周に濠をめぐらして、寺院そのものは3層の回廊で構成されている。中央に65メートルにおよぶおおきな塔があり、四隅にちいさい塔がある。中央の塔には階段状に石づみがつくられているので、塔の上部までのぼることができる。ただ、おそろしく傾斜が急なので、わたしは足がすくんで途中であきらめた。寺院の各所にはおおきな神像があって、参拝するひとがあとをたたない。回廊のすそにはおどる女神たち、アプサラスの群像をはじめ、ラーマーヤナの物語の各場面をあらわす浮きぼりがほどこされている。

3層の回廊の壁面には無数の落書きがある。数百年のあいだに、この寺に参詣した人たちが記念にかきのこしていったものである。さまざまな文字でしるされているが、なかには漢字でかかれた日本語のものもある。

そのひとつに、肥州の住人森本右近太夫一房の署名があった。熊本のひとである。寛永9（1632）年の日付がある。この当時は鎖国まえで、御朱印船が多数くりだして、東南アジアの各地には日本人町が形成されていた。カンボジアにも、プノムペンのちかくにウドンという日本人町があったという。森本右近太夫も御朱印船による訪問者であったのであろう。かれはこの壮麗な寺院をみて、祇園精舎にきたとおもったらしい。アンコールの研究家の石澤良昭氏によれば、そのころ日本国内で祇園精舎の絵図面として流布していたものは、まぎれもなくこのアンコール・ワットのそれであったという。森本右近太夫の誤解はむりからぬものであった。

祇園精舎というのは、「平家物語」の冒頭にある「祇園精舎の鐘の声、諸行無常のひびきあり」でよく知られているように、南アジアの仏教の一大センターとかんがえられていた。もちろんそれは、今日のインドのウッタル・プラデシュ州にあったもので、アンコール・ワットとは別ものである。

アンコール・ワットは、今日では南方上座部仏教の寺院である。それはスリランカにはじまり、中世以後に東南アジア諸国に導入されてひろまったものである。ビルマもタイもカンボジアもラオスも、現在ではすべて上座部仏教になっている。アンコール・ワットは創建当時はヒンドゥー教の寺院であった。古代の東南アジアは仏教よりも、おしなべてヒンドゥー教につよい影響をうけていたのである。

カンボジア国家の建国伝説によると、インドからバラモン教の高僧のカウンディニヤというひとがやってきた。そのころカンボジアには女王がいたが、彼女は全裸であったという。カウンディニヤはこの女王をとらえて妻として、自分はこの国の王になった。裸体は野蛮の象徴であり、バラモン僧は高度の文明をあらわしている。ここにインド文明による古代国家が建設されたのであった。

古代の東南アジアには、高度に発達したインド文明の影響のもとに成立した諸国家群がならんでいた。タイ西部のドヴァーラヴァティやスマトラのシュリーヴィジャヤ、それから派生したジャワのシャイレンドラなどである。クメール国家もそのひとつで、いちばん東には、いまのベトナム南部にチャンパとよばれる国があった。いずれもインド文明の影響のもとに組織された国で、フランス人の歴史学者ジョルジュ・セデスによって「インド化された国ぐに」と名づけられたものである。これらの国は、現在においては南方上座部仏教かイスラーム、あるいは大乗仏教におきかわっているが、もともとはすべてヒンドゥー教であった。「インド化された国ぐに」は、また「ヒンドゥー化された国ぐに」であったのである。

ヒンドゥーの理念によって建立されたアンコール・ワットの祭神は、もとよりヒンドゥーの神であった。アンコール・ワットの中央の塔奥の上部にまつられている神はヴィシュヌ神である。同時にヒンドゥーの観念には、デーヴァラージャすなわち「神なる王」ということがあった。あるいは王が神なのである。アンコールの主塔にまつられたヴィシュヌ神は、同時にその建立者スーリヤヴァルマン2世にほかならない。

日本にはヒンドゥー教がはいってくることはなかった。しかし、「インド化された国ぐに」がヒンドゥー国家群として形成されるまえから、日本はすでに仏教化していた。6世紀なかばには、朝鮮半島から仏教が伝来していたのである。ただし、この仏教は東南アジア諸国における南方上座部仏教ではなく、アジア大陸の中央部をとおってもたらされたところの大乗仏教であった。

しかし、そこにもインドにおいて形成された「神なる王」の観念はつたえられていたはずである。じっさいに日本国家においても王が神であるという観念は、仏教によってはじめてもたらされたものであろう。その意味では、仏教によって文明化されたいわゆる海東諸国家も、またひろい意味での「インド化された国ぐに」の一種であったと見ることもできるであろう。そうだとすれば、8世紀なかばにおける奈良の大仏の鋳造と大仏殿の建立は、まさにのちのアンコール・ワットの建立に比すべきできごとであったのかもしれない。そして、アンコール・ワットのヴィシュヌ神が建立者のスーリヤヴァルマン2世そのひとであったように、奈良の大仏すなわち巨大な毘廬遮那仏（びるしゃなぶつ）は、建立者である聖武天皇そのひとではなかったかとおもわれる。

国立民族学博物館顧問

Tadao Umesao

In 1860, French explorer Henri Mouhot "discovered" the existence of splendid stone buildings in the jungle of Northwest Cambodia. This was the so-called "discovery of Angkor Wat." The existence of this temple was already known to some Europeans, but it became famous in Europe through Mouhot's descriptive introduction.

The existence of these great buildings was also, of course, very well known to the Cambodians who lived in the area, but the buried portion had never been excavated. It was surrounded by forest, but the building itself was exposed above ground.

I visited this splendid temple for the first time in 1957. I was also there again in the Spring of the following year. What I can say for sure from my two visits is that Angkor Wat is not a ruin. It is a living, functioning temple. Actually there were monks of the Theravada Buddhist sect living there in that place of faith and incense burned uninterrupted. Such a living religious establishment must not be treated as a ruin.

Angkor Wat was built around the beginning of the twelfth century, and its construction, under king Suryavarman II, took 30 years. Adjacent to Angkor Wat are the ruins of Angkor Thom. This is undoubtedly a deserted ruin, with a group stone structures remaining. It was the royal palace of the Khmer empire of the Angkor dynasty, and was built under Khmer king Jayavarman VII during the late 12th and early 13th centuries. This was the capital of the Khmer state and the Angkor dynasty at the height of its power on the Indochina peninsula. I drove around the area in a jeep, and there were ruins throughout the thick forest. Just a superficial survey was a full day's work.

Returning to Angkor Wat, this huge temple has a moat around its periphery, and the temple itself is constructed with galleries on three levels. In the center stands a tower of 65 meters, and there are small towers at the four corners. The central tower is built with stones stacked to form terraces, so it is possible to climb to the top, but the incline is very steep and my legs failed me midway. Throughout the temple there are statues of gods, and there is a constant stream of worshipers. Many relief carvings of dancing goddesses, apsaras, and scenes from the Ramaayana are displayed throughout the panels of the gallery walls.

There are writings scrawled everywhere in the three gallery levels. These writings commemorate the visits of pilgrims over the centuries. The writings appear in various scripts including one entry in Japanese characters.

This one entry was signed by one Morimoto Ukondayu Kazufusa, a resident of Hishuu. He was from Kumamoto. The entry was dated 1632. This was before Japan's period of self-isolation, and many trading vessels authorized by the shogunate visited the ports of South East Asia where Japanese communities were established. In Cambodia, near Phnom Penh there is said to have been a Japanese town called Udon. Morimoto Ukondayu Kazufusa probably traveled on one of the authorized trading vessels. He probably saw this magnificent temple and thought he had arrived at Gion shrine. According to Angkor scholar Yoshiaki Ishizawa, pictures of the Gion shrine were circulating in Japan at the time, and he says they were undoubtedly pictures of Angkor Wat. The mistake by Morimoto Ukondayu Kazufusa is understandable.

The Gion shrine is mentioned in the beginning of the well

known Tale of the Taira Clan — "The bell of Gion shrine tolls, all things flow and nothing is permanent" — and was thought to be a major center of Buddhism in South Asia. Of course it is now known to be in India's Uttar Pradesh and not Angkor Wat.

Angkor Wat is now a Southern Theravada Buddhist temple. This branch of Buddhism began in Sri Lanka and spread by introduction to the nations of South East Asia from the middle ages. The Buddhism of Burma, Thailand, Cambodia and Laos is also Theravada Buddhism. At the time when Angkor Wat was created, it was a Hindu temple. In ancient times, Hinduism generally had a stronger influence than Buddhism in South East Asia.

According to the legend of Cambodia's formation, a Brahman named Kaundinya came from India. At that time in Cambodia there was a queen, and she was naked when she met Kaundinya. Taking the queen for his wife, he became king. Her nudity symbolizes nature, while his status as Brahman represents high civilization. In this way, the culture of India gave rise to the establishment of the ancient state.

Ancient South East Asia was made up of a group of states established under the influence of a highly developed Indian culture. Dvaravati of western Thailand, Srivijaya of Sumatra, and the derivative Shailendra of Java are examples. The Khmer state is another example, and the furthermost eastern example of this was the country called Champa in the south of present day Vietnam. All of these nations were organized under the influence of Indian culture, and they were called "Indianized states" by French historian George Cœdès. These nations are now Theravada Buddhist or Islamic, or they have converted to Mahayana Buddhism, but they were all originally Hindu. They were "Indianized states" or "Hinduized states."

According to Hindu thought, the enshrined deity of Angkor Wat was originally a Hindu god. The god enshrined in the upper interior of Angkor Wat's central tower is Vishnu. The contemporary Hindu concept of devaraja, or "god king" deified the king, and the Vishnu god enshrined in the main tower of Angkor is none other than Suryavarman II who had it constructed.

The Hindu religion never came to Japan. Japan had already become Buddhist before the "Indianized nations" had been formed as Hindu states. Buddhism was conveyed to Japan from the Korean peninsula in the middle of the sixth century. However, this was not the Theravada Buddhism of South East Asia, but the Mahayana Buddhism from the central Asian continent.

However, the concept of the "god king" that had been established in India was conveyed there, too. Actually, the concept of the king being a god that is present in the Japanese state probably had its origins in Buddhism. In this light, the eastern seaboard states that flourished under Buddhism can probably be seen in the broad sense as "Indianized nations." If that is so, then the casting of the great Buddha and the establishment of the temple of the great image of Buddha in Nara in the middle of the eighth century may be events comparable to the later establishment of Angkor Wat. And, as Suryavarman II who had constructed Angkor Wat was the Vishnu god, so I might suppose that the Shomu emperor who established the great Buddha of Nara (the great Birushanabutsu) may have been that god.

Special Advisor of The National Museum of Ethnology

ヘレン・イビッソン・ジェサップ

夜明け前、アンコール・ワットの尖塔は薄藍色の熱帯夜を背景にその形をわずかにとどめているに過ぎない。しかし、夜明けの息吹が空を淡紅色に染めると、遺跡をほのかに取り巻く薄もやが姿を現わし、太陽は、鬱蒼と繁った寺院背後の森からその最初の黄金の瞬きを中央聖堂の高峰から注ぎ始める。壁や回廊を照らし次第に塔の下へと太陽がその光を滑らせ、穏やかな橙色から金色へと輝きを増し、この夜明けのドラマの終焉に、遺跡がその華麗な全貌を初めて見せる。これを目にする時、人は超越的な想いに駆られずにはいられない。

この暁のロマンス以外に日没のアンコール・ワットを好んで見る人も多いが、夜明けや日暮れが背景に無くとも、塔が遺跡前の儀式用水池にその姿を映すアンコール・ワットには圧倒されるものがある。古代エジプトのピラミッドに見られる偉業や、ジャワのボロブドゥールの持つ造形、彫像、精神性の見事な融和に、人は畏敬の念を抱くものである。聖ペテロのバシリカ聖堂における物体と空間の勝ち誇ったかのような調和や、引力を否定してそびえるシャルトル聖堂が創出する心的高揚にも我々は驚嘆するばかりである。これらは全て人類最高の造形的偉業であり、理想の表現が技術と合体しかつ技術を超越しているものである。然し、象徴性、構造、規模の完璧なる融合においてアンコール・ワットを凌ぐものは無いのではないか。アンコール・ワットの建造者達が存在観念の全てを実現させるには時間と運動法則が不可欠な要素であることを認識していたことに見る人が気付いた瞬間、アンコール・ワットのその空間が広がりを持ち始め精神の高揚を覚える。啓示を受けたこれら建造者達は、人間の手で空間における可能性を完全に具現化させる構想を抱いたのだ。

9世紀末からクメール王朝の首都であったアンコールのこの驚くべき建築傑作は西暦1131年、スーリヤヴァルマン2世王朝時代（1107から1150年）に建立された。この建物の方角は、ほとんどのクメール寺院が東方に向かって建てられているのとは対照的に、西の方向、即ち死の方角に向かって建てられていることから、おそらく王の葬儀の寺院として機能を果たしていたと考えられる。ヴィシュヌ派のヒンドゥー寺院として建立されているため建立王はスーリヤヴァルマン2世であったとわかるが、14世紀後は仏教の寺院として神聖化されてきた。中央部は約2キロ四方の囲い地になっており、その環濠には高い列柱で支えられ手すりの突端に首をもたげたナーガ蛇頭を配した歩道が一本横渡しになっている。この半キロに及ぶ参道は同心の回廊で囲まれた中庭へと続き、中庭には中央部の聖所に最も高い塔、四隅に4基の塔、合計で5基の尖塔がそびえ、その中央塔はカンボジアの最も偉大なこの聖山の最高峰となっている。

これまでの宗教建造物の中でも最大の偉容を誇るアンコール・ワットは、宇宙を建築物という形で表現しようとしたクメールの試みにおいてその頂点を成すものだ。インド文化の影響を受けた国々、特にカンボジアにおいて、聖山はヒンドゥーの神々の宿であり、彼等の宇宙の中心であるメール山（須弥山）のシンボルとして見られてきた。宇宙の中心メール山が水で囲まれているように、聖山も宇宙の海を表わしている水で囲まれている。現在では人工湖、西バライの城壁が一部残るばかりの廃墟となっているアクヤムの小規模寺院で始まる初期クメールの聖山に対する表現は、この人工貯水池が掘られた11世紀当時はその規模がそれほど大がかりなものではなかった。アクヤムは3層のピラミッドで7世紀から8世紀の間に建立されたものである。

カンボジアの継承君主はそのほとんどが寺院を建立しているが、この中に聖山が含まれており、それらは国の寺院で守護紳に奉納さ

れ、アンコール・ワットに見られるように通常5基の塔で囲まれ5層のピラミッド型を成している。12世紀のアンコール・ワット以前のものとしては、精気溢れるバコン寺院（前アンコール時代の首都で現在はロリュオスとなっているハリハララヤで881年に建立）、次いでアンコール内に建設された、バクヘン（907年に奉納）、プレループ（961年）、タケオ（975年前後）、バプオン（1060年前後）等がある。最後の聖山はバイヨンで12世紀末、ジャヤヴァルマン7世時代の首都アンコール・トムに物心両面の中心地として建立されている。慈悲心溢れる柔和な観世音菩薩面が彫られた49に及ぶ塔は、感動的な宗教像で人の心を包み込むものだ。こういったクメール建築から得られる強烈な3次元経験を2次元表現に置き換えるのは至難な業であるにもかかわらず、井津建郎の洞察力に満ちた作品はその空間美を見事に写真平面上に表現した。

　化粧しっくいを施した煉瓦から始まり、ラテライトそして最終的には砂岩へと発展し、時には3種類の材料の組み合わせとしても見られる、これら見事な熟練技に、クメールの完全巧みな様式技術が表われている。精巧に彫りの入った列柱や片蓋柱、複雑な唐草模様と神聖な人物や動物画が施されたリンテル（目草）、物語風情景のあるペディメント（破風）、扉、疑似扉、欄干付き窓、精緻な枠に囲まれ中に守護神像の入った壁龕等は、その大きさを建造物に対し大胆に取りながらも同時に緻密な要素を構成している。バンテアイ・スレイのリンテルとペディメントの生命力や繊細な窓格子から、様々な姿で舞う美しい髪飾りの天女、アプサラスを描く優雅で創意に富んだ深い浮き彫りから、さらに1キロ近くにわたってアンコール・ワットの回廊に見られる叙事詞英雄達の彫刻群に至るまで、様々な驚くべき浮き彫りによって、早くも7世紀には、タケオ郡のサンボア・プレイ・コク寺院群の壁はその芸術的高みへとすでに到達していた。同時にクメールの芸術家達は、壁などの浮き彫り

以外にも優雅でヒューマニズムに富んだ一体一体の彫刻像、ロンデ・ボス、の創作においても並み外れた才能を見せている。

　クメールの建築及び彫刻に見られるインド文化の明らかな影響は、歴史上かなり早くから始まった両者の交流を反映するものだ。伝説として語り継がれるものは別として、5〜6世紀のものである最古の碑文以前のカンボジア史について知るには、中国と進貢または交易関係にあった国々が示されている中国王朝の記録に頼らなければならない。概略ではあるがこれらの記録に出てくる国々の中に、扶南、真鑞という二つの国が中国語の音訳で記述されており、今日のカンボジアの南北にあたる地域を占めていたと考えられる。前者は海運、後者は農業が主体の国だったようだ。さらに中国の旅行家、ジューダクアン（Zhou Daguan -- 英語の旧式では Chou ta Kuan 又は Tchcou Ta Kuan）の回顧録から、14世紀におけるカンボジアの生活も知ることができる。

　東南アジアにおける初期の国々については一般に充分に理解されていない。紀元前2000年あるいはもっと古くから、現在の中国南西地域からの人口移動というよりは、ゆったりとした流浪による東南アジア地域へのオーストロネシア民族の流入が起きていた。国として形成されつつあった当初、これらの地域は中央による厳しい管理もない市場を中心とした比較的自由な構造で成り立っていたと考えられる。扶南「王朝」はオクエオの地を中心にそういった形で形成されていたものと思われる。中国の記録には、オクエオは高度に発展した水路のある城壁を巡らした都市で、高床式の家々には豊かな金の装飾物を身に付けた優雅な住民が住んでいたと記されている。

　扶南は、東南アジアにおいて最も早くインドとヌインドを通じて地中海地方と交易のあった地域で、オクエオ地域から発見された紅玉髄宝石や日付け入り銀貨など考古学的遺品から、遠く離れたローマ帝国と交流があったことが確認できる。カンボジアの誕生を語る

神話は、カウンディニャと呼ばれるバラモンが海を渡って現われ、王国を制覇した後、蛇王、ナーガの娘、ソマと結婚したと伝えている。この伝説はインドとクメール文化における民族融合を象徴するものとして解釈できるが、それは、同様の伝説が現代の中央ベトナムにあった古代チャンパ王国に存在していたことからもうなずける。

一方、より確実な歴史を把握するならば、古くはサンスクリット語、7世紀以降はクメール語も加わって書かれた碑文が刻まれているカンボジア発見の石碑によることができる。これら碑文はほとんど一貫して宗教的内容を呈し、インド文明の最も明らかな影響であったヒンズー教と仏教という2大宗教の寺院に関連がある。守護紳に保護を求めた王の祈願文、王家の系図の記述、さらには王の功績が書かれており、それらは自画自賛の形ではあるが、歴史的な背景を知る手がかりとなる。表面がサンスクリット語になっている石碑の裏面にクメール語が刻まれていることがよくあり、その内容は寺院の土地や動産などを列挙したもので、サンスクリット語よりも単調な形で書かれており、宗教生活のより組織的な面を伺い知ることができる。

碑文は寺院から発見されることが多く、寺院は主に当時の支配者によって建立されたものであることから、我々が知り得るカンボジアの過去は主に王室の歴史に限られることになる。特に王位継承が長子相続制に固執しなかった王朝における動乱は頻繁で、非宗教的な建築物は王室のもの平民のものを問わず腐敗しやすい建材で作られた故、古くに消滅しているため、クメール王朝の系図は宗教的建造物やその碑文からしか知ることができない。王が12世紀にチャンパ民と戦った様子がバヤン寺院の浮き彫りに描かれているように、浮き彫りには歴史的な事件が描写されているということがよくある。一方クメールの日常生活に関しては、唯一これら寺院回廊の下

層に記された詳細な描写から知ることができる。王や守護神が象あるいはナーガの首を頂部に装飾した乗り物に意気揚々と乗っている姿、また戦士を乗せて戦いに向かい水路を堂々と進む長い船などが、レリーフの上部パネルに描かれているが、その下方には、魚を料理している様子、パンを焼いている者、女達がしゃべっている姿、闘鶏試合を観戦している人混みなど、日常生活の様子が描写されている。またこれらの浮き彫りからは、カンボジアにおける非宗教的な建築様式をも知ることができる。これらの建築は優美に彫刻された柱や屋根のひさしにその特性があったことが伺える。

近隣諸国による領地奪回やカンボジア内における王子達のライバル国建設などによって、縮小したこともあったが、ジャヤヴァルマン2世が802年にカクラバーティンとして、あるいは宇宙の支配者として即位宣誓を行って以来、クメール王国は徐々に拡大していった。何人かの王の治世下では、今日のタイ、ラオス、および中央ベトナムのチャンパから成る王国が形成されていた。12世紀末、ジャヤヴァルマン7世は僧院や病院の広範にわたるネットワークを設立し、近隣諸国にまで延びる道路および橋などを建設した。12世紀から13世紀初頭における壮大な絵巻風浮き彫りの時代までには、クメールの支配を証拠付ける王の勅令布告を記す石碑や石柱を、東はタイのロプブリ、北はラオスのバットビューに至るまで発見することができる。しかし、この支配は、その後に起きた植民地の歴史の中で考えられるような統治組織ではなく、むしろ部族間の緩やかな結合であったと想定される。

今日、クメール文明といえばアンコールを通常思い起こすが、カンボジアの建築及び彫刻における天才達の足跡はアンコール以外国内の多方面で発見することができ（例えば、11世紀における北のプレアビヒア、7世紀における南のサンボァプレイ・コク建造物）、1000年以上も続いた高い文化がいかに広範に浸透していたかを証明

するものである。タイがアンコールを征服した後も、プノンペンから統治されることとなったカンボジア王朝は、彫刻と建築の伝統を守り続け、その絶頂期の王朝時代ほど卓越したものではないにしても、特に木彫の伝統において、優れた品質を示している。

保存上の欠陥、コーベルアーチ（持送りアーチ）使用に由来する構造的な脆弱さ、さらには生い茂る樹木の浸食が重なって、今日、人類が持つ最も貴重な芸術遺産の一つがその存続を危ぶまれている。森林の侵略というロマンス、蛇のような樹根と優艶なる破風や片蓋柱との異様な共生が創出する非現世的な美は、これら建築の天才達の無比なる表現にさらなるドラマを与えている。この超現実的なドラマは、井津建郎の写真によってその時間と空間が凝縮され永遠なる記録としてここに残されることになった。

美術史家

Spirit of Place: The Genius of The Khmers

Helen Ibbitson Jessup

Just before dawn the towers of Angkor Vat are mere shadows etched against the paling indigo of the tropical night. The first hint of dawn washes the sky with pink and reveals delicate mists wreathing the stones. The sun rises behind the temple's luxuriant forest and the first rays gild the pinnacle of the central sanctuary. Gradually the light slides down the towers, bathing the walls and galleries, and strengthens from apricot to gold as the sun enriches the spectrum until the great monument glows from within. It is a transcendental experience.

Even without the romance of sunrise, or the more frequently watched sunset, when the towers are reflected in the ceremonial pools in front of the monument, Angkor Vat is overwhelming. We are awed by vast achievements like the pyramids of ancient Egypt and by the inspired blend of iconography, form and spirituality of Java's Borobudur. We marvel at the triumphant harmony of mass and spatial rhythm in St. Peter's basilica and at the exaltation negating gravity in Chartres cathedral. All embody humankind's highest plastic achievements, where the expression of an ideal merges with and transcends technique. But none surpasses Angkor Vat, with its perfect fusion of symbolism, structure and scale. Here the spirit soars, as the three dimensions are expanded by the awareness that the elements of time and motion were envisaged as essential for the fulfilment of the context: the inspired architect has orchestrated a scheme that depends on human participation for the full realization of the spatial potential.

This astonishing architectural masterpiece in Angkor, the capital of the Khmer kingdom from the end of the ninth century, was dedicated in 1131 AD during the reign of Suryavarman II (r. 1107 - ca. 1150). Its orientation is westward, the direction of death, in contrast to the eastward-facing situation of most Khmer temples, which indicates its probable function as a funerary temple for the monarch. It was dedicated as a Hindu temple to Visnu, with whom Suryavarman II was identified, but since the fourteenth century has been consecrated as a Buddhist temple. Its central enclosure area is approximately a mile square, its encircling moat crossed by a high colonnaded causeway with balustrades terminating in rearing naga heads. This quarter-mile ceremonial way leads to a series of concentric galleried courtyards rising to a central group of five towers, one at each corner and the highest, the central sanctuary, forming the peak of Cambodia's grandest temple mountain.

Angkor Vat, the most magnificent religious structure ever conceived, is the apogée of Khmer attempts to represent the universe in architectural form. In countries influenced by Indic culture, and in particular in Cambodia, the temple mountain was seen as the symbol of Mt. Meru, the home of the gods of the Hindu pantheon and the center of their universe. Like that universe it was surrounded by water representing the cosmic ocean. Earlier Khmer expressions of the temple mountain were on a less ambitious scale, beginning with the small temple of Ak Yum, now a total ruin partly displaced by the rampart of the artificial lake, or west baray, when that reservoir was excavated in the eleventh century. It was a three-level pyramid built sometime between the seventh and eighth century.

Successive Cambodian monarchs typically constructed temples of which one, the state temple dedicated to a protective deity, was a temple mountain, usually of five levels in pyramid form surmounted by a group of five towers, as at Angkor Vat. Such powerful monuments as Bakong (dedicated in 881 in the pre-Angkor capital of Hariharalaya, now Roluos), and then in Angkor itself, Bakheng (dedicated in 907), Pre Rup (961), Ta Keo (around 975) and Baphuon (around 1060) preceded the twelfth-century Angkor Vat. The last temple mountain was Bayon, built at the end of the twelfth century as the physical and spiritual centre of Jayavarman VII's capital city of Angkor Thom. Its forty-nine towers carved with the calm face of the Bodhisattva Lokesvara radiating benevolence in all four cardinal directions comprise the heart of another of the world's most compelling religious images. The unforgettable spatial experience of Khmer architecture challenges pictorial representation, but the insightful photographs of Kenro Izu offer compelling visual evidence of its beauty.

In their evolving mastery first of brick with stucco decorations, then of laterite and finally of sandstone, and sometimes in a combination of all three materials, the Khmers demonstrated consummate formal and technical skills. Finely chiselled colonettes and pilasters, lintels with intricate garlands and hieratic personages and animals, pediments with narrative scenes, doors, false doors, balustered windows and elaborately framed niches housing guardian figures offer detailed elements in confident proportion to the scale of the monument. As early as the seventh century, on the walls of the group of Sambor Prei Kuk in Takeo province, the temples were enhanced by extraordinary bas reliefs ranging from the delicate tracery and vitality of Banteay Srei's lintels and pediments, through the graceful inventiveness of deeper relief showing apsaras, or celestial dancers, in myriad poses and fantastic headdresses, to the architectonic sweep of the sculptured epics on Angkor Vat's galleries, almost half a mile in length. At the same time Khmer artists demonstrated outstanding talent in the carving of free-standing, or ronde-bosse, sculpture of unparalleled iconic grace and humanism.

The Indian cultural influences that are apparent in Khmer architecture and sculpture reflect contacts that began early in our era. For information about Cambodian history before the oldest known local inscriptions of the fifth and sixth centuries, apart from what is enshrined in legend, we must draw on Chinese dynastic records of contacts with states that had a trading or tributary relationship with the empire. Among the states mentioned in these records, which are sketchy, are two that are represented in Chinese transliteration as Funan and Zhenla and that seem to have occupied the south and north of the area that is roughly present-day Cambodia. They seem predominantly to have been, respectively, maritime and agricultural states. We can also learn of life in Cambodia in the fourteenth century from the memoirs of the Chinese traveller, Zhou Daguan (formerly Chou ta Kuan or Tcheou Ta Kuan).

The nature of early states in Southeast Asia is not fully understood. Austronesian migrations, or rather, the gradual drifting of Austronesian peoples to the Southeast Asia region from an area that is now the southwest of China occurred from an early period, probably two thousand years or more before our era. The emerging states were probably loosely structured at first, without tight central control, and focussed around market centers. It is thought that the Funan "kingdom" centered at Oc Eo was so constituted. Chinese records describe Oc Eo as a walled city with developed waterways, houses on stilts and prosperous inhabitants who wore rich gold ornaments.

Funan was one of the earliest regions in Southeast Asia to have trading relations with India and thence with the Mediterranean area, and some of the archaeological finds such as carnelian jewellry and dated silver coins from digs in the Oc Eo area confirm these far-flung relationships with, among others, the Roman Empire. Cambodian myths of origin tell of a Brahman called Kaundinya who arrived by sea, conquered the kingdom then married Soma, the daughter of the ruling serpent, or naga, king. This legend could be seen as symbolising the fusion of Indic and indigenous elements in Khmer culture, the more convincingly since a similar legend was preserved in the ancient kingdom of Champa in modern Central Vietnam.

We are on more certain historical ground with stone inscriptions found in Cambodia, the earliest being carved in Sanskrit verse but from the seventh century also incised in the Khmer language. The information in these inscriptions is almost exclusively religious and connected with temples serving the two great religions, Hinduism and Buddhism, that were the most visible influences of Indian civilization. One can read kings' requests to a patron deity for protection and descriptions of their genealogies as well as accounts of these monarchs' achievements that furnish some kind of historical background, albeit couched in self-flattering terms. Khmer inscriptions, often found on the obverse side of a stele where the front face is incised in Sanskrit, are more prosaic, listing temple lands and chattels and the like and offering some insight into the organization of religious life.

Since the evidence of epigraphy tends to be found in temples, and since these were usually built by rulers, our knowledge of the Cambodian past is largely confined to royal history. Dynastic upheavals were frequent (especially since royal succession did not adhere to primogeniture) and as secular architecture, whether for kings or commoners, was made of perishable materials and has long since disappeared, it is only through sacred structures and their inscriptions that we can piece together the genealogies of the Khmer kings. Occasionally bas reliefs illustrate historic events, as when the reliefs on the Bayon temple depict the king's twelfth-century battles against the inhabitants of Champa. It is from details on the lower registers of these galleries that we derive our only insight into the daily life of the Khmers. Below the upper panels of relief where monarchs and deities ride in triumph on elephants or in palanquins with naga-head finials, or where long ships sweep through the water carrying troops to battle, the sculptors depicted domestic scenes where fish is cooked, bread is baked, women chat and crowds watch cockfights. From these reliefs we learn also about the form of secular architecture in Cambodia; it seems to have been characterised by elegantly carved columns and roof eaves.

Starting with the proclamation of Jayavarman II as cakravartin, or ruler of the universe, in 802, the kingdom of the Khmers gradually expanded, although at times it also retracted as neighbouring states resumed conquered territory or as local princes set up rival states within Cambodia. Under several of its monarchs the kingdom comprised parts of present day Thailand and Laos as well as of Champa in central Vietnam. At the end of the twelfth century Jayavarman VII established a wide network of hermitages and hospitals, roads and bridges that stretched into neighbouring countries. By the era of the great narrative reliefs, that is to say, the twelfth and early thirteenth centuries, evidence of Khmer authority could be found on stele proclaiming royal edicts as far east as Lopburi in Thailand and as far north as Vat Phu in Laos. This authority, however, was probably expressed in a loose tributary relationship rather than a governing organization such as we might postulate from the evidence of later colonial history.

Although today we usually think of Khmer civilization in terms of Angkor, evidence of Cambodian architectural and sculptural genius is found in many other parts of the country (the eleventh-century Preah Vihear in the north, for example, and the seventh-century structures of Sambor Prei Kuk in the south), attesting to the pervasive nature of the high culture that was sustained for over a thousand years. Even after the Thai conquest of Angkor, the Cambodian dynasties that subsequently ruled from Phnom Penh continued a tradition of sculpture and architecture, that while not as sublime as when the empire was at its zenith, was nevertheless of impressive quality, particularly in the continuing traditions of wood sculpture.

Today the combination of neglect, the structural weakness inherent in the use of the corbelled arch and the mighty invasion of strangling trees all threaten the survival of one of mankind's most precious artistic heritages. The romance of the forest's invasion, the unearthly beauty of the strange symbiosis of snake-like roots and noble pediments and pilasters lend this unequalled expression of architectural genius an added drama that is memorably captured by the inspired photography of Kenro Izu.

Art Historian

作品は、すべてプラチナ・パラジウム・プリントで、
図版25と26を除き、
サイズは33.2cm×48.5cmです。

The original photographs of this catalog are
platinum-palladium prints.
Image size - 14 inch x 20 inch,
except plate #25 & #26 as indicated.

1. アンコール #4, アンコール・ワット
   Angkor #4, Angkor Wat, 1993

2. アンコール #88, アンコール・ワット
   Angkor #88, Angkor Wat, 1994

3. アンコール＝21, アンコール・ワット
Angkor =21, Angkor Wat, 1993

4. アンコール #29, アンコール・ワット
   Angkor #29, Angkor Wat, 1993

5.　アンコール＝134, アンコール・ワット
　　Angkor #134, Angkor Wat, 1994

6. アンコール＝136, アンコール・ワット
   Angkor =136, Angkor Wat, 1994

7. アンコール =93, アンコール・ワット
   Angkor =93, Angkor Wat, 1994

8. アンコール=107, アンコール・ワット
   Angkor =107, Angkor Wat, 1994

9. アンコール=155, タ・プローム
Angkor =155, Ta Prohm, 1994

10. アンコール#26, タ・プローム
Angkor #26, Ta Prohm, 1993

11. アンコール =193
タ・プローム
Angkor #193
Ta Prohm, 1995

12. アンコール#158, タ・プローム
Angkor #158, Ta Prohm, 1994

13. アンコール #78, タ・プローム
    Angkor #78, Ta Prohm, 1994

14. アンコール＃87, タ・プローム
Angkor #87, Ta Prohm, 1994

15. アンコール=16, タ・プローム
    Angkor #16, Ta Prohm, 1993

16. アンコール=2, タ・プローム
Angkor #2, Ta Prohm, 1993

17. アンコール=8, タ・プローム
Angkor =8, Ta Prohm, 1993

18. アンコール＝3, タ・プローム
    Angkor =3, Ta Prohm, 1993

19.　アンコール＝15, タ・プローム
　　　Angkor ＝15, Ta Prohm 1993

20. アンコール =190, タ・プローム
Angkor =190, Ta Prohm, 1995

21. アンコール＝70, タ・プローム
   Angkor =70, Ta Prohm, 1994

22. アンコール =221, タ・プローム
Angkor =221, Ta Prohm, 1995

23. アンコール=14, タ・プローム
    Angkor =14, Ta Prohm, 1993

24. アンコール＝71, タ・プローム
Angkor ＝71, Ta Prohm, 1994

25. アンコール＝208，タ・プローム
    Angkor #208, Ta Prohm, 1995
    53.3 cm x 106.7 cm

26. アンコール#122, タ・プローム
Angkor #122, Ta Prohm, 1994
71.8 cm x 101.6 cm

27. アンコール #111, プラサット・クラヴァン
Angkor #111, Prasat Kravan, 1994

28. アンコール #205, プレ・ループ
Angkor #205, Pre Rup, 1995

29. アンコール＝10, ニャック・ポアン
　　 Angkor ＝10, Neak Pean, 1993

30.　アンコール＝120, ニャック・ポアン
　　Angkor =120, Neak Pean, 1994

31. アンコール #168, プリヤ・パリライ
Angkor #168, Preah Palilay, 1995

32. アンコール #224
    プリヤ・パリライ
    Angkor #224
    Preah Palilay, 1995

33. アンコール=84, バコン
　　Angkor =84, Bakong, 1994

34.　アンコール#95, バコン
Angkor #95, Bakong, 1994

35.　アンコール#149, タ・ソム
　　Angkor #149, Ta Som, 1994

36. アンコール #147, タ・ソム
Angkor #147, Ta Som, 1994

37. アンコール=151, タ・ソム
Angkor #151, Ta Som, 1994

38 アンコール=219, タ・ソム
Angkor =219, Ta Som, 1995

39. アンコール=175, 東メボン
Angkor =175, Eastern Mebon, 1995

40. アンコール＝187
東メボン
Angkor ＝187
Eastern Mebon, 1995

41. アンコール＝202, 東メボン
Angkor ＝202, Eastern Mebon, 1995

42. アンコール≠180, 東メボン
Angkor ≠180, Eastern Mebon, 1995

43. アンコール #131, プリヤ・カン
Angkor #131, Preah Kahn, 1994

44. アンコール =197
プリヤ・カン
Angkor =197
Preah Kahn, 1995

45. アンコール=30, プリヤ・カン
Angkor =30, Preah Kahn, 1993

46. アンコール=31, プリヤ・カン
Angkor #31, Preah Kahn, 1993

47.　アンコール＝24
　　　プリヤ・カン
　　　Angkor ＝24
　　　Preah Kahn, 1993

48. アンコール＝20, プリヤ・カン
Angkor ＝20, Preah Kahn, 1993

49. アンコール=72, プリヤ・カン
Angkor =72, Preah Kahn, 1994

50. アンコール=89, プリヤ・カン
    Angkor =89, Preah Kahn, 1994

51. アンコール =199, プリヤ・カン
Angkor =199, Preah Kahn, 1995

52. アンコール=132, プリヤ・カン
    Angkor #132, Preah Kahn, 1994

53. アンコール=127, プリヤ・カン
Angkor =127, Preah Kahn, 1994

54.　アンコール＝6, バンテアイ・スレイ
Angkor =6, Banteay Srei, 1993

55. アンコール＝12, バンテアイ・スレイ
Angkor =12, Banteay Srei, 1993

56. アンコール #11, バンテアイ・スレイ
   Angkor #11, Banteay Srei, 1993

57. アンコール=179, スラ・スラン
   Angkor =179, Srah Srang, 1995

58. アンコール=143, スラ・スラン
   Angkor =143, Srah Srang, 1994

59. アンコール＝96，バイヨン
Angkor ＝96, Bayon, 1994

60. アンコール=73, バイヨン
Angkor #73, Bayon, 1994

61. アンコール＝74, バイヨン
Angkor =74, Bayon, 1994

62. アンコール#195
バイヨン
Angkor #195
Bayon, 1995

63. アンコール＝185
　　バイヨン
　　Angkor =185
　　Bayon, 1995

64. アンコール≠182
バイヨン
Angkor ≠182
Bayon, 1995

65. アンコール＝79, バイヨン
Angkor #79, Bayon, 1994

井津建郎　略年譜

1949年	大阪に生まれる
1969〜71年	日本大学芸術学部　写真学科
1971年	渡米
1974年	ニューヨークにてスティル・ライフ・スタジオ開設
1979年	石造遺跡の撮影を始める
1981年	キャッツキル写真センター奨学金を受ける
1983年	プラチナ・パラジウム・プリントを始める
1984年	アメリカ連邦政府美術奨学金を受ける
1985年	ニューヨーク州美術基金奨学金を受ける

■ 主な個展

1983年	フォトファインド・ギャラリー(ウッドストック、ニューヨーク)
1985年	キャッツキル写真センター(ウッドストック、ニューヨーク)
1986年	アート・アウェアネス・ギャラリー(レキシントン、ニューヨーク)
1987年	アン・リード・ギャラリー(ケッチャム、アイダホ) フォトファインド・ギャラリー(ニューヨーク)
1990年	フォト・フェスト／イノヴァ・ギャラリー(ヒューストン、テキサス)
1991年	ツァイト・フォトサロン(東京) アン・リード・ギャラリー(ケッチャム、アイダホ) ピクチャー・フォト・スペース(大阪)
1992年	ハワード・グリーンバーグ・ギャラリー(ニューヨーク) マイケル・シャピロ・ギャラリー(サンフランシスコ) ツァイト・フォトサロン(東京)
1993年	サウスイースト写真美術館(デイトナ・ビーチ、フロリダ) ギャラリー・ザ・ストッカレック(チューリッヒ) A.O.Iギャラリー(サンタフェ、ニュー・メキシコ)
1994年	ハワード・グリーンバーグ・ギャラリー(ニューヨーク) フェリッシモ・ギャラリー(ニューヨーク) ツァイト・フォトサロン(東京) フェロモン・サロン・ド・アート(ハリウッド)
1995年	アン・リード・ギャラリー(ケッチャム、アイダホ)
1996年	清里フォトアートミュージアム(清里) マイケル・シャピロ・ギャラリー(サンフランシスコ) ジャクソン・ファイン・アーツ(アトランタ、ジョージア)

■ コレクション

ボストン美術館

カナダ建築センター、モントリオール

サンフランシスコ近代美術館

ヒューストン美術館

サウスイースト写真美術館、デイトナ・ビーチ、フロリダ

メトロポリタン美術館、ニューヨーク

清里フォトアートミュージアム

スミソニアン・インスティテューション

ロサンジェルス郡立美術館

Biography

1949	Born in Osaka, Japan
1969-1971	At Nihon University, College of Art, major in Photography
1971	Moved to New York City
1974	Established Kenro Izu Studio
	Became freelance photographer
1981	Received Catskill Center for Photography Fellowship
1983	Began platinum-palladium printing
1984	Received National Endowment of Arts
1985	Received New York Foundation of Arts

■ Selected Solo Exhibitions

1983	Photofind Gallary, Woodstock, NY
1985	Catskill Center for Photography, Woodstock, NY
1986	Art Awareness Gallery, Lexington, NY
1987	Anne Reed Gallery, Ketchum, ID Photofind Gallery, New York
1990	Photo-Fest/Inova Gallery, Houston, TX
1991	Zeit Foto Salon, Tokyo Anne Reed Gallery, Ketchum, ID Picture Photo Space, Osaka
1992	Howard Greenberg Gallery, New York Michael Shapiro Gallery, San Francisco Zeit Foto Salon, Tokyo
1993	Southeast Museum of Photography, Daytona Beach, FL Gallerie Zür Stockeregg, Zurich, Switzerland A.O.I. Gallery, Santa Fe, NM
1994	Howard Greenberg Gallery, New York Felissimo Gallery, New York Zeit Foto Salon, Tokyo Pheromone Salon d'Art, Hollywood
1995	Anne Reed Gallery, Ketchum, ID
1996	Jackson Fine Arts, Atlanta, GA Kiyosato Museum of Photographic Arts, Kiyosato Michael Shapiro Gallery, San Francisco

■ Selected Collections

Boston Museum of Fine Arts

Canadian Center for Architecture

San Francisco Museum of Modern Art

Houston Museum of Fine Arts

Southeast Museum of Photography

Metropolitan Museum of Art

Kiyosato Museum of Photographic Arts

Smithsonian Institution

Los Angeles County Museum

プラチナ・プリントとは

　プラチナ・プリント(Platinum Print)とは、銀塩の代わりに鉄塩の感光性を利用し、塩化白金と鉄塩の感光液を水彩画用紙等に塗布した印画紙を、乾燥後、太陽光か紫外線灯光でネガを密着焼き付けて画像を得るタイプをいう。白金を用いた画像は黒のしまりがよく、階調の幅が広く、グレーの調子がほとんど無限に表現でき、耐久性が優れていることが特徴である。白金の還元作用については1800年初頭から知られていたが、いわゆるプラチナ印画紙として登場するのは、1873年イギリスのウィリアム・ウィリス(William Willis)によって発表されたものである。1880年代、90年代に多くの写真家が使用し名作を残したが、その後は、引き伸ばし可能な銀塩を用いた印画紙が製品化され、普及したこと、そして第一次世界大戦によるプラチナの高騰にともなってこの技法も徐々に下火となった。現代になって、均一生産化した印画紙に対抗するべく、個性的な表現テクニックのひとつとして、各種の古典的な印画法が着目されはじめ、プラチナ・プリントはそのひとつとして再び利用されている。

　プラチナ・プリントの精緻で微妙なトーン、銅版画のようなきめの細かさは、フィルムと紙の密着焼きにより、その本領を発揮する。プラチナは紫外線のみに感光するため、また乳剤の感度が非常に低いため、引伸機にかけることは不可能なのである。

　井津建郎は、1979年から古代遺跡の撮影を始めて3年目の1981年、オークションの下見会でポール・ストランドのプラチナ・プリントを手にした瞬間、それが古代遺跡を表現するのに最適の技法と確信した。以来数年間、試行錯誤が続いた。そして、重さ百キロにもなる14×20インチの大型カメラと大判フィルムを特注し、同サイズのネガを作り、14×20インチの密着焼きプリントの製作を可能とした。

　このような大判サイズのネガ現像処理の難しさもさることながら、特にプリンティングにおいては、多くの要素が結果に影響を及ぼす。プラチナとパラジウムの混合比率によっても階調や色調が変わるうえに、感光剤を紙に塗る時の時間のかけ方、湿気と温度の関係、乾燥の仕方でも様々に変わる。さらに感光剤との化学反応を防ぐために、紙にあらかじめ施されているサイジング(下びき)処理やpH調整(中性)処理を取り除くための、紙の前浴処理を行わなければならない。井津建郎は、こうした技法を自らのものとしたと思われる現在でも、出来上がったプリントがすべて満足のいくものというわけにはいかないと語る。

Platinum Prints

Platinum prints are photographs made with a process that uses ferrous salts instead of silver salts. For the process, water color or printing paper is coated with a light sensitive solution of platinum chloride and ferrous salts. After drying, it is contact printed with a negative using sun or ultraviolet light. The blacks in images made using platinum are fine, and gradation is wide with grey elements that are nearly unlimited. The images are also permanent.

The platinum reducing process was known around the beginning of the 1800s, but the platinum print first appeared in 1873 with the work of William Willis. It was used in many of the surviving works of photographers of the 1880s and 90s, but with the proliferation of products using silver salts, and with the boost in platinum prices during World War I, the technique gradually declined. Recently, various classic printing techniques have gained notice, and platinum prints are again being made by photographers who resist the uniformity of mass produced printing papers and who seek a novel medium of expression.

By contact printing with film and paper, platinum prints exhibit their special subtlety and delicate tones. Since platinum is sensitive only to ultraviolet light, and since the emulsion sensitivity is extremely low, it cannot be used with enlargers.

In 1979, Kenro Izu began photographing ancient stone monuments. Two years later, in 1981, at a preview for an auction at Sotherby's he saw a platinum print by Paul Strand, and at that moment he was convinced he had found the best medium for presenting stone monuments. For Izu there followed some years of trial and error. He ordered large 14" by 20" custom camera equipment that in total weighs 200 pounds, and custom film of the same size. With these negatives he creates 14" by 20" contact prints.

Processing of such a large format negative is difficult, and for printing in particular, many factors affect the result. Changes in the ratio of platinum and palladium will cause variations in contrast and tone. Further variations are brought about by adjusting the coating time of the paper with light sensitive material, and the relationship between humidity and temperature. There are even various methods for drying. Furthermore, to avoid chemical reactions with the light sensitive material in the paper, surface treatment and pH adjustment processes are performed prior to coating. Even though Izu has now mastered this technique, he often has to reject resulting prints which do not meet his exacting standards.

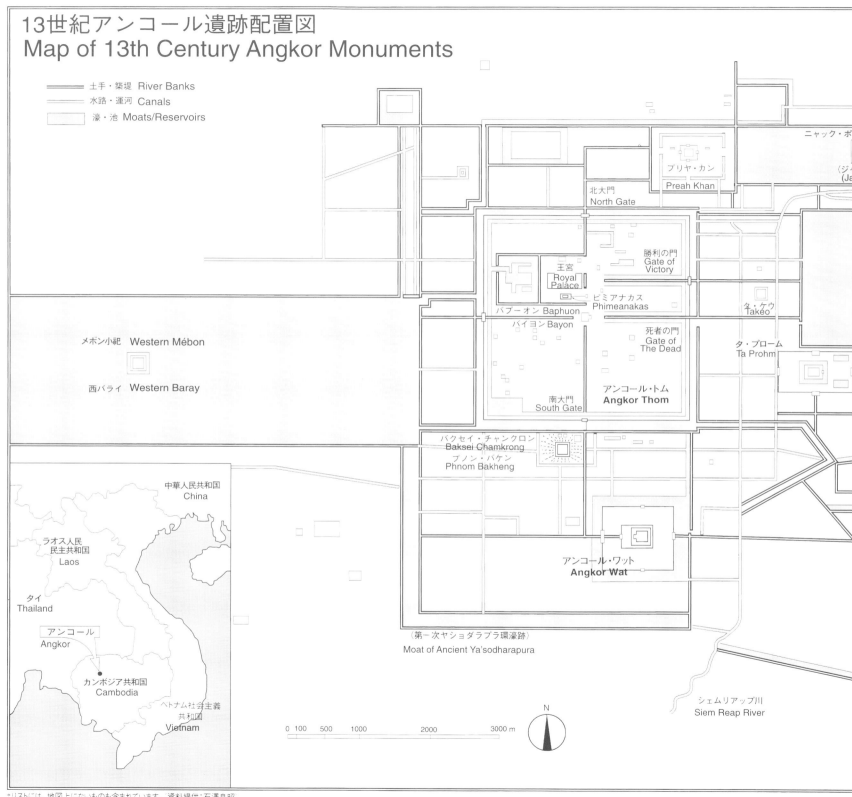

13世紀アンコール遺跡配置図
Map of 13th Century Angkor Monuments

土手・築堤 River Banks
水路・運河 Canals
濠・池 Moats/Reservoirs

ニャック・ポ
(ジャ
(Ja

プリヤ・カン
Preah Khan

北大門
North Gate

勝利の門
Gate of
Victory

王宮
Royal
Palace

ピミアナカス
Phimeanakas

タ・ケウ
Takeo

バプーオン Baphuon

バイヨン Bayon

死者の門
Gate of
The Dead

タ・プローム
Ta Prohm

メボン小祠　Western Mébon

アンコール・トム
Angkor Thom

西バライ　Western Baray

南大門
South Gate

バクセイ・チャンクロン
Baksei Chamkrong

プノン・バケン
Phnom Bakheng

中華人民共和国
China

ラオス人民
民主共和国
Laos

アンコール・ワット
Angkor Wat

タイ
Thailand

アンコール
Angkor

（第一次ヤショダラプラ環濠跡）
Moat of Ancient Ya'sodharapura

カンボジア共和国
Cambodia

ベトナム社会主義
共和国
Vietnam

0　100　500　1000　2000　3000 m

N

シェムリアップ川
Siem Reap River

*リストには、地図上にないものも含まれています。資料提供：石澤良昭
*The list includes places not on the map. (references provided by Yoshiaki Ishizawa)

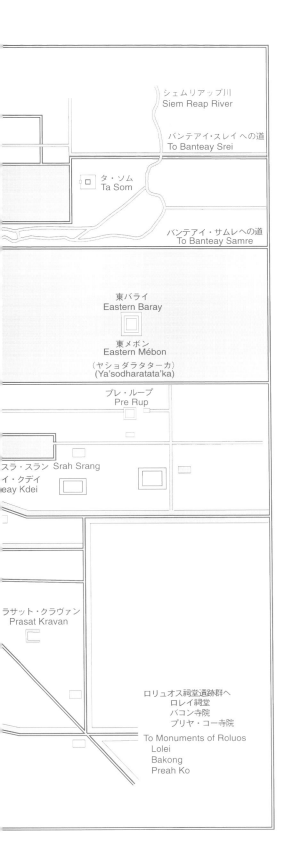

シェムリアップ川
Siem Reap River

バンテアイ・スレイへの道
To Banteay Srei

タ・ソム
Ta Som

バンテアイ・サムレへの道
To Banteay Samre

東バライ
Eastern Baray

東メボン
Eastern Mébon

（ヤショダラタターカ）
(Ya'sodharatata'ka)

プレ・ループ
Pre Rup

スラ・スラン Srah Srang

イ・クデイ
eay Kdei

ラサット・クラヴァン
Prasat Kravan

ロリュオス祠堂遺跡群へ
ロレイ祠堂
バコン寺院
プリヤ・コー寺院

To Monuments of Roluos
Lolei
Bakong
Preah Ko

■ 主要遺跡紹介

アンコール・ワット (Angkor Vat)
建立年代：1113～1145年頃
建立王：スーリヤヴァルマン2世
宗教：ヒンドゥー教(ヴィシュヌ派)
規模等：環濠(南北1.3km×東西1.4km・幅190m)。正面の西参道は540m。中央塔(高さ65m)を中心にした五基の尖塔で有名。三重の回廊があり、第一回廊(東西200m×南北180m)には全面に絵巻物のごとき薄肉彫りの浮き彫りがある。クメール建築の調和と円熟を示している。1632年、日本人森本右近太夫一行が訪れた。

アンコール・トム (Angkor Thom)
建立年代：12世紀末～13世紀初め
建立王：ジャヤヴァルマン7世
宗教：仏教(観世音菩薩)
規模等：一辺3kmの正方形、5つの城門、8mの高さの周壁、環濠。「大きな町」の意。1431年頃、シャム(タイ)軍の侵入を受けて放棄した。4面仏顔塔は世界に類例がない。

バイヨン寺院 (Bayon)
建立年代：12世紀末
建立王：ジャヤヴァルマン7世
宗教：仏教(観世音菩薩)
規模等：高さ45m。アンコール・トムの中心寺院。多数の塔には合計196面の観世音菩薩の面が彫られている。第一、第二回廊には、アンコール・ワット回廊より深い浮き彫りがある。題材は従来のヒンドゥー教のものが多い。

バプーオン寺院 (Baphuon)
建立年代：1060年頃
建立王：ウダヤーディティヤヴァルマン2世
宗教：ヒンドゥー教(15世紀以降は仏教寺院に)
規模等：「隠し子」の意。第二次アンコール王都の中心寺院。西側に改修された寝釈迦像がある。

ピミヤナカス寺院 (Phimeanakas)
建立年代：10世紀末～11世紀初め
建立王：スールヤヴァルマン1世
宗教：ヒンドゥー教
規模等：紅土の三層の基壇の上に砂岩で造られた擬似小回廊がある。

象のテラス (Terrasse des éléphants)
建立年代：12世紀末
建立王：ジャヤヴァルマン7世
宗教：仏教 (観世音菩薩)
規模等：南北350m、高さは中央部と両端が4m、中間部は3.5m。壁全面に象の彫刻がある。

ライ王のテラス (Terrasse du Roi Lépreux)
建立年代：12世紀末
建立王：ジャヤヴァルマン7世
宗教：仏教 (観世音菩薩)
規模等：高さ約6m×一辺約25。南東部は曲がりくねった二重の壁がある。テラスには高さ約1mのライ王の座像 (レプリカ) がある。

タ・ケウ寺院 (Ta Kev)
建立年代：1000年頃
建立王：ジャヤヴァルマン5世
宗教：ヒンドゥー教(シヴァ派)
規模等：周壁は東西120m×南北100m。「ケウの古老」の意。未完成のまま放棄されているため、往時の建築手順の検証が可能である。砂岩の組石の精密さに注目したい。従来のピラミッド寺院に、新たに回廊が加えられている。

タ・プローム寺院 (Ta Prohm)
建立年代：1186年
建立王：ジャヤヴァルマン7世
宗教：仏教(観世音菩薩)
規模等：「梵天の古老」の意。王が母の菩提を弔うため建立された。発見当初のまま保存され、荒れ果てた境内やスポアン(バンヤン樹 榕樹)の大木には驚かされる。密林のなかの遺跡の様子を伝えている。

バンテアイ・クデイ寺院 (Banteay Kdei)
建立年代：12世紀末
建立王：ジャヤヴァルマン7世
宗教：仏教(ヒンドゥー教の様式との混淆あり)
規模等：東西700m×南北500m。スラ・スラン浴地に隣接。複雑な平面展開をなしている。上智大学が調査・研究・現場研修を実施している。

プラサット・クラヴァン寺院 (Prasat Kravan)
建立年代：921年
建立王：ハルシャヴァルマン1世
宗教：ヒンドゥー教
規模等：横に並んだ5つの祠塔。中央の塔以外は上部が前壊しているが、そのままの状態で保存修復した。主建材はレンガとラテライト。レンガ上に直接ラクシュミー女神の浮き彫りが施された。B.Ph.グロリエが1962年に修復工事を開始。新旧のレンガが使用されているが、両者を区別するため新しいレンガには◎のマーク(Conservation-保存事務所の意)が入っている。

スラ・スラン (Srah Srang)
建立年代：12世紀末
建立王：ジャヤヴァルマン7世
宗教：仏教(観世音菩薩)
規模等：東西700m×南北300m。「水浴の池」の意。砂岩の縁取り、西側のテラスはジャヤヴァルマン7世治下だが、掘削はそれ以前に行われた。ポル・ポト治下、水田にされてしまった。

プレ・ループ寺院 (Pre Rup)
建立年代：961年
建立王：ラージェンドラヴァルマン2世
宗教：ヒンドゥー教(シヴァ派)
規模等：基壇と周壁はラテライト、祠堂はレンガ、祠堂の四隅の壁龕には漆喰の女神デヴァター像が見られるが、一部剥落している。

東メボン祠堂 (Mébon Oriental)
建立年代：952年
建立王：ラージェンドラヴァルマン2世
宗教：ヒンドゥー教(シヴァ派)
規模等：東バライ貯水池の中心部に建立された、三層のピラミッド型寺院。四隅の象の彫刻が有名。

タ・ソム寺院 (Ta Som)
建立年代：12世紀末
建立王：ジャヤヴァルマン7世
宗教：仏教(観世音菩薩)
規模等：東西200m×南北240mの周壁。もともと僧院であった。壁龕(へきがん)には美しい女神像がある。前壊がはげしい。

ニャック・ポアン寺院 (Neak Pean)
建立年代：12世紀末
建立王：ジャヤヴァルマン7世
宗教：仏教(観世音菩薩)
規模等：「絡みあう蛇」の意。中央大池と4つの小池がある。中央祠堂の基壇には、尾を絡ませた2匹の大蛇の彫刻があり、仏教的宇宙観を具現した遺跡である。

プリヤ・カン寺院 (Preah Phan)
建立年代：1191年
建立王：ジャヤヴァルマン7世
宗教：仏教(観世音菩薩)
規模等：「聖なる剣」の意。東西800m×南北700mの環濠、三重の周壁。第一周壁には四方にそれぞれ3つの塔門があり、塔門脇の紅土壁に浮き出したガルーダ(神鳥)像がナーガ(蛇)を捕まえている。

プノン・バケン寺院 (Phnom Bapheng)
建立年代：900年頃
建立王：ヤショヴァルマン1世
宗教：ヒンドゥー教(シヴァ派)
規模等：高さ60mの自然の小丘の上に立つ高さ47mの寺院。プノン・クロム、プノン・ボックと並ぶアンコール3聖山の一つ。第一次アンコール王都(10世紀初め)の中心。

ロリュオスの遺跡群 (Roluos)
アンコールに遷都される以前の王都。790年頃ジャヤヴァルマン2世がひらいたといわれる。

バコン寺院 (Bakong)
建立年代：881年
建立王：インドラヴァルマン1世
宗教：ヒンドゥー教(シヴァ派)
規模等：一辺700m×幅60mの環濠をめぐらした、最初のピラミッド型寺院。5層の基壇の壁面には、美しい浮き彫りが施されていたと考えられるが、現在ではほとんどが剥離。ハリハラ神(シヴァ神とヴィシュヌ神の合体神)立像が有名。

ロレイ祠堂 (Lolei)
建立年代：893年
建立王：ヤショヴァルマン1世
宗教：ヒンドゥー教(シヴァ派)
規模等：インドラタターカ大貯水池の中心の小島に建てられたが、現在では池の水は枯れている。4基の祠堂が残っているが、損壊が著しい。上座部仏教の寺院がすぐ脇に建てられている。

バンテアイ・スレイ寺院 (Banteay Srei)
建立年代：967年
建立王：ラージェンドラ2世、ジャヤヴァルマン5世(実質上はジャヤヴァルマン5世の摂政を務めたバラモン高僧で王師であるヤジュニヤヴァラーハ)
宗教：ヒンドゥー教(シヴァ派)
規模等：「女の砦」の意。アンコールの宝玉と呼ばれるほど、彫刻・文様・浮き彫りには注目すべきものがある。「東洋のモナリザ」と呼ばれた女神浮彫りは有名。マルローの小説『王道』(1930年)のモデル。

バンテアイ・サムレ寺院 (Banteay Samre)
建立年代：12世紀中頃
建立王：スールヤヴァルマン2世
宗教：ヒンドゥー教(ヴィシュヌ派)
規模等：「サムレ(入れ墨)族の砦」の意。ミニ・アンコール・ワットといわれている。この寺院にまつわるキュウリ作りから王になった男の伝説がある。

西バライ (Western Baray)
建立年代：11世紀後半
建立王：ジャヤヴァルマン6世
規模等：東西8km×南北2km×深さ4～5mの大貯水池。現在はシェムリアップ空港がすぐ脇にある。灌漑のための水がめで、乾季に近隣の田地へ水を供給するために掘られた。

■ Major Monuments:

Angkor Wat
Erected: c. 1113 to 1145
Erected by: Suryavarman II
Religion: Hindu (Vishnu sect)
Scale, etc.: Moat (1.3 km north-south, 1.4 km east-west, 190 m wide). Front western approach is 540 m. Famous for its five terminal towers with the central tower standing 65 m high. It has triple peripheral galleries; all surfaces of the first peripheral gallery (200 m east-west, 180 m north-south) have picture scroll-like low bas reliefs. This monument displays the harmony and perfection of Khmer architecture. In 1632, the Japanese, Morimoto Ukondayu Kazufusa, visited.

Angkor Thom
Erected: Late 12th to early 13th centuries
Erected by: Jayavarman VII
Religion: Buddhist (Kanzeon Bosatsu)
Scale, etc.: Square with sides 3 km in length, five gates, outer walls 8 m high with moat. Means "Large City." It was abandoned after an invasion by the Siam (Thai) army around 1431. These four sided Buddha face towers cannot be found anywhere else in the world.

Bayon
Erected: Late 12th century
Erected by: Jayavarman VII
Religion: Buddhist (Kanzeon Bosatsu)
Scale, etc.: Standing 45 m high, it is the central temple of Angkor Thom. On its many towers, there are a total of 196 faces of the Kanzeon Bosatsu carved. In its first and second peripheral galleries there are bas reliefs carved deeper than at Angkor Wat. Much of the subject matter comes from Hinduism of the earlier period.

Baphuon
Erected: c. 1060
Erected by: Utyadityavarman II
Religion: Hindu (From the 15th century it became a Buddhist temple)
Scale, etc.: Means "Hidden Child." It was the central temple of the second Angkor capital. On the west side is a restored, sleeping Buddha.

Phimeanakas
Erected: Late 10th to early 11th centuries
Erected by: Suryavarman I
Religion: Hindu
Scale, etc.: There is a small false gallery built of sandstone on a three-level laterite terrace foundation.

Terrace of Elephants
Erected: Late 12th
Erected by: Jayavarman VII
Religion: Buddhist (Kanzeon Bosatsu)
Scale, etc.: Measures 350 m north-south; height at center and both ends is 4 m and 3.5 m in between. There are elephant carvings on all wall surfaces.

Terrace of the Leper King
Erected: Late 12th
Erected by: Jayavarman VII
Religion: Buddhist (Kanzeon Bosatsu)
Scale, etc.: Measures about 6 m high with each side about 25. On the south-east corner there is a meandering double wall. At the terrace there is the seated Leper King (a replica) of about 1 m in height.

Takeo
Erected: c. 1000
Erected by: Jayavarman V
Religion: Hindu (Shiva sect)
Scale, etc.: Outer walls measure 120 m east-west and 100 m north-south. Means "Ancestor Keo." Since it was abandoned in an unfinished state, it is possible to study the construction procedure. The precision fit of the sandstone is remarkable. The new peripheral galleries were additions to the earlier pyramid temples.

Ta Prohm
Erected: 1186
Erected by: Jayavarman VII
Religion: Buddhist (Kanzeon Bosatsu)
Scale, etc.: Means "Ancestor Brahma." Erected by the king in worship to the Buddha for the happiness of the soul of his mother; it has been left as it was found with the grounds in a remarkable state of disrepair and overgrown by large bayan trees. It conveys the aspect of ruins in the middle of a dense jungle.

Banteay Kdei
Erected: Late 12th century
Erected by: Jayavarman VII
Religion: Buddhist (mixed with Hindu forms)
Scale, etc.: Measures 700 m east-west and 500 m north-south. It is adjacent to Srah Srang bathing place and uses complicated surface development. Sophia University is conducting surveys and on-site research.

Prasat Kravan
Erected: 921
Erected by: Harshavarman I
Religion: Hindu
Scale, etc.: Five shrine towers stand side by side. While the upper portion of all but the central tower have collapsed, they have been repaired and preserved as they were found. The main building material was brick and laterite. Directly above the brick there is a bas relief- of the goddess Lakshmi. Bernard-Philippe Groslier began restoration in 1962. New and old bricks have been used; in order to distinguish between the two, a "c" (for Conservation) with a circle was used to mark the new bricks.

Srah Srang
Erected: Late 12th century
Erected by: Jayavarman VII
Religion: Buddhist (mixed with Hindu forms)
Scale, etc.: Measures 700 m east-west and 300 m north-south. Means "Bathing Pond." Bordered by sandstone, the west side terrace was created under Jayavarman VII, but the digging was conducted earlier. Under Pol Pot it became a water-filled paddy.

Pre Rup
Erected: 961
Erected by: Rajendravarman II
Religion: Hindu (Shiva sect)
Scale, etc.: Foundation terraces and outer walls are laterite, shrine towers are brick. Mortar statues of devatas can be seen at the four corners of the shrine towers, but they are severely deteriorated

Eastern Mébon
Erected: 952
Erected by: Rajendravarman II
Religion: Hindu (Shiva sect)
Scale, etc.: Erected in the central portion of Eastern Baray reservoir, this is a three level pyramid shaped shrine. The elephant statue carvings on the four corners are famous.

Ta Som
Erected: Late 12th century
Erected by: Jayavarman VII
Religion: Buddhist (Kanzeon Bosatsu)
Scale, etc.: Peripheral walls are 200 m east-west and 240 m north-south. This was originally a temple. There are beautiful goddess statues recessed in the walls. Deterioration is severe.

Neak Pean
Erected: Late 12th century
Erected by: Jayavarman VII
Religion: Buddhist (Kanzeon Bosatsu)
Scale, etc.: Means "Twining Serpents" It has a large central pond and four small ponds. At the base of the central tower there is a carving of two large snakes with their tails intertwined; this ruin embodies the Buddhist sense of space.

Preah Kahn
Erected 1191
Erected by: Jayavarman VII
Religion: Buddhist (Kanzeon Bosatsu)
Scale, etc.: Means "Sacred Sword." Surrounded by three successive walls and a moat that extends 800 m east-west and 700 m north-south. On the first wall, each of the four surrounding walls has three gates, and on the laterite walls by the gates, Garuda birds appear in relief holding Naga serpents.

Phnom Bakheng
Erected: c. 900
Erected by: Yashovarman I
Religion: Hindu (Shiva sect)
Scale, etc.: This temple of 47 m in height stands on a natural hill of 60 m in height. It is one of three sacred hills that include Phnom Krom and Phnom Bok. This is the central mountain of the first Angkor king (at the beginning of the 10th century).

Roluos
The former capital prior to its transfer to Angkor. Jayavarman II is said to have established it around 790 A.D.

Prah Ko
Erected: 879
Erected by: Indravarman I
Religion: Hindu (Shiva sect)
Scale, etc.: This is a temple with six shrine towers erected for the parents of the king. The name means "Sacred Cow," and derives from the three sacred figures of Nandin placed facing in worship of the monument. Of the Angkor ruins that can be dated, this is the oldest. The monument extends 500 m east-west and 400 m north-south. Erection inscriptions still remain on the inner walls.

Bakong
Erected: 881
Erected by: Indravarman I
Religion: Hindu (Shiva sect)
Scale, etc.: Surrounded by a moat whose sides measure 700 m in length and 60 m in width, this was the first pyramid shaped temple. On the wall surfaces of the five-level foundation terraces there probably were beautiful bas relief-s but they are almost completely stripped away. There is a famous statue of Hari Hara (the combined deities of Shiva and Vishnu).

Lolei
Erected: 893
Erected by: Yashovarman I
Religion: Hindu (Shiva sect)
Scale, etc.: Built on a small island in the center of Indratataka reservoir that is now dry. Four shrine towers remain, but damage is conspicuous. A Theravada Buddhist temple has been built nearby.

Banteay Srei
Erected: 967
Erected by: Rajendravarman II, Jayavarman V (actually Yajnavaraha who served in a regency as a high official and guru for Jayavarman V)
Religion: Hindu (Shiva sect)
Scale, etc.: Means "Fortress of Women." Known as the jewel of Angkor for its carvings, designs and bas relief-s. There is a famous bas relief- of a goddess known as "Asia's Mona Lisa." This was the model for Malraux's "The Royal Way" (1930).

Banteay Samre
Erected: Mid 12th century
Erected by: Suryavarman II
Religion: Hindu (Vishnu sect)
Scale, etc.: Means "Fortress of the Samre (tattoo) Tribe." It is called the mini-Angkor Wat. There is a legend surrounding this temple about a man who went from growing cucumbers to become a king.

Western Baray
Erected: Second half of the 11th century
Erected by: Jayavaruman VI
Scale, etc.: A large reservoir measuring 8 km east-west, 2 km north-south, and 4 to 5 meters deep. The Siem Reap airport now stands nearby. It was an irrigation reservoir that was dug so that water could be distributed to fields in the dry season.

(References provided by Yoshiaki Ishizawa)

フレンズ・ウィズアウト・ア・ボーダーとそのアンコール・チャイルド・クリニック・ファンドについて
About "Angkor Clinic for Children" and "Friends Without A Border"

カンボジアでは1940年代以来、およそ800万個にものぼる地雷が埋められています。4万人を越える一般市民が死亡、或いは負傷し、今日でも被害は続き、野原で遊ぶ子供達が犠牲者となることも頻繁です。また、医療設備の不足により、日本や西欧諸国では稀になった小児病の犠牲者も少なくありません。フレンズ・ウィズアウト・ア・ボーダーは、カンボジアの子供達の負傷、病気を無料で治療する"アンコール・チャイルド・クリニック"建設を目指して活動しています。

フレンズ・ウィズアウト・ア・ボーダーは、1995年に写真家・井津建郎により創設されたアジアの子供達を救うことを目的とするニューヨーク州認可の非営利団体です。主なメンバーは、写真家、インダストリアル・デザイナー、画廊経営者、大学教授、美術館学芸員、編集者、建築家、グラフィック・デザイナーで構成されています。

井津は、ニューヨーク在住の古代遺跡写真家として、約17年間に亘り、エジプト、シリア、ヨルダン、メキシコ、イギリス、スコットランド、フランス、チリ（イースター島）、ビルマ、インドネシア、カンボジアを特注の14インチ×20インチ（33.2cm×48.5cm）のカメラで撮影を続けてきましたが、過去3年間、6度のアンコール・ワット、及びその周辺遺跡群の撮影を通して、今までにはない、心に響く大切なことを学ばせてもらったような気がすると言います。また、不運にも地雷の犠牲になった子供達を見て、何か彼にできることがあれば、このアンコール遺跡の村に感謝の気持を表現させてほしいという思いが募り、アンコール・チャイルド・クリニック・ファンドの設立に到りました。これらの子供達の命を救うことを願って、アンコール．ワット遺跡群写真の売り上げ金をその基金に充て、一億円を目標に、日本・アメリカ・ヨーロッパ各地で、チャリティー展覧会を催す企画を現在進めています。展覧会では、写真、写真集及びカードの販売とともに、企業スポンサーや個人の寄付という形での協力も得られれば幸いです。これらの展覧会は、壮麗なアンコール・ワット遺跡の美しさとその影に潜む、遺跡破壊に通じる組織化された美術品盗難、及びカンボジアの歴史と惨事についての知識を恵まれた国の人々に広める良い機会にもなります。

戦争、そして社会の疲弊による皺寄せは、いつも罪のない子供達に最も大きくかかってくるようです。カンボジアの傷ついた子供達のために私達皆で暖い気持ちを贈りたいと思います。世界中の子供達に、我々は皆友達なのだと意識を持ってもらうことが将来の平和な社会を築く礎となることと信じます。皆様の御支援と御協力のもとに、一日も早く病院が完成されることを願います。

Tokyo office：フレンズ・ウィズアウト・ア・ボーダー
〒153 東京都目黒区中目黒5丁目1番18号　松島彰雄方　Tel/fax. 03-5722-2381

銀行振込：東京 三菱銀行・新赤坂支店　普通預金口座1006207
フレンズ・ウィズアウト・ア・ボーダー

An estimated eight million land mines have been planted in Cambodia since the 1940's. Forty thousand civilians have been injured or killed, and people continue to be injured every day. Among the victims are innocent children at play in the fields. Also, due to insufficient medical facilities, there are victims of pediatric diseases which are obsolete in Japan and most Western countries. *Friends Without A Border* is building the *Angkor Clinic for Children* to provide much needed free aid to these injured and sick children.

Founded in 1995 by photographer Kenro Izu and registered in New York State, *Friends Without A Border* is a non-profit organization with the sole objective of saving the lives of Asian children. Board Members and Advisory Board Members include photographers, industrial designers, art gallery owners, a college professor, publicity agent, architect, curator, editor and graphic designer.

Kenro Izu is a New York based photographer, and photographing ancient stone monuments around the world is one of his major fine art interests. Over the past seventeen years he has traveled the world with his custom-made 14" X 20" camera photographing monuments in Egypt, Syria, Jordan, Mexico, England, Scotland, France, Chile (Easter Island), Burma, Indonesia, and Cambodia.

Izu has traveled to Cambodia six times in the last three years, and the experience has been deeply moving. Having witnessed the tragedy firsthand, he feels it is imperative that he does something to help the children who have fallen victim to the land mines. Raising funds for the *Angkor Clinic* is Izu's way of expressing appreciation to the Angkor Monument, which has profoundly touched his heart. Toward this end, Izu has established a fund from the sales of his Angkor Monument photographs. To reach the goal of raising one million dollars, benefit shows will be held throughout the United States, Japan, and Europe. These shows will also serve to educate people in more fortunate countries about the tragedy of Cambodia and its history, as well as the beauty of the magnificent Angkor monuments and the associated crisis - the organized theft of artifacts from the monuments.

New York Office: Friends Without A Border
140 West 22nd Street, Suite 11A, New York, NY 10011
tel. 212-254-1002　fax. 212-255-9060

Cambodia Office: Seung Kong
14 EO Rue de la Croix Rouge
Cambodgienne, Sangkath Boeng Raing, Phnom Penh, Cambodia
tel. 015-912-108　fax. 23-427-897 (receiving only)